The Foothold

Written by:

Joseph R. Adomavicia and Lauren Howard

This book was written to help find the footholds in our lives that we need to get from the bottom of this soul crushing mountain to the pinnacle of our very existence.

Book design by Joseph R. Adomavicia and Lauren Howard.

Published Independently.

This book is dedication to you. The readers. The ones who are taking a step forward. The ones who are working to better themselves. The ones who have decided to stick their foot out and take a hold of their life. No longer accepting what is and attempting what can be. You owe it to yourselves, and we owe it to you.

The Foothold

HAVE YOU SETTLED?

ARE YOU CONTENT?

HAVE YOU FINISHED?

THEN YOU'VE

GIVEN UP!

Satisfaction

'Is that all you're looking for?'

I dread this word. Satisfaction to me is conceding to the fact that you never really got what you wanted. You may be satisfied, but still not pleased. Being content with our lives is one of the biggest mistakes we can make as human beings. We should never fight for satisfaction. We should never be satisfied, period. We strive for greatness, for unbeatable achievement. Satisfaction tricks the brain to think it doesn't need to go any farther. Us, we never stop. We always press on. For bigger and greater things. There is no end to this drive we worked so hard to acquire. There is no finish line. There are only miles ahead and we just need to keep creating that fuel. The fuel that lights the fire inside of us, keeping us driven to work harder, get smarter, and shatter our goals. When we become satisfied, we die inside. Convincing ourselves that we've done enough. Only to watch others surpass us on their way to a higher standard and a more fulfilling life. With satisfaction we have no meaning. All we have is the encumbering truth that we accepted defeat and can now lie to ourselves and say, 'this is all I wanted'. But it's not. We want more. We want life. Nothing should be able to make us fight, only to receive...

Satisfaction.

IT ALL STARTS WITH YOU.

Quench Your Thirst

Ask yourself, what in this life brings you satisfaction?
What keeps your heart beating and your blood pumping?
Is it the dream job?
Is it the massive mounds of money?
Or is it the love and lust that tastes sweet like honey?
Well, whatever it is, just don't stop desiring.
Quench your thirst, and then ask yourself,
what in this life brings you satisfaction?
What keeps your heart beating and your blood pumping?
Is it the rush of fast cars and jet planes?
Is it the wind in your face while cruising on your Harley?
Or is it that need to travel, unveiling the unknown?
Well, whatever it is, just don't stop desiring.
Quench your thirst, and then ask yourself,
what in this life brings you satisfaction?
What keeps your heart beating and your blood pumping?
Is it the success of your family?
Is it the success of your friends?
Or is it the fulfillment of having your own?
Well, whatever it is, just don't stop desiring.
Quench your thirst, and then ask yourself,
what in this life brings you satisfaction?
Is it the crunch of autumn leaves beneath your feet?
Is it the sun, sky, and breeze of a Spring afternoon?
Or is it the cherry blossoms carried by the winds?
Or is it the way snowflakes fall gracefully to the ground?
Well, whatever it is, just don't stop desiring.
Quench your thirst, and then ask yourself,
what in this life brings you satisfaction?

Share Your Story
About The
#Satisfaction_Foothold
@The_Foothold

Scan and Watch
Author Reading
and Commentary

ANTICIPATE
THE
NEXT
MOVE

Initiative

'Do you know the next move?'

Then what are you waiting for? Do it! Don't doubt yourself. Go for it. If you fail, You're better off. Next time, you won't! You've just gained more knowledge. More confidence. We all need more confidence! We can't just sit on the sidelines waiting for things to get done for us. We must take action. Believe in ourselves. We certainly can't do that by waiting. If you don't know the next move. Look for it. Learn more about it. Ask! Get familiar. And don't stop there. Start to think ahead. 10 steps ahead! When someone is on step 1, they are working toward step 2. Start working on step 3 and 4. Preparing for step 5. Think of step 10 while working on all of the steps leading up to it. Never focus solely on that individual moment. When you are about to jump, do you look down? Or just jump? You can't keep acting while being near sighted. Yet, you must act! There isn't a place for those who sit around hoping someone else will think ahead for them. We do this ourselves. In our actions, we prepare for the next. The more we do this, the more confident we grow in our each and every action. Leading us to be better, faster, more efficient, and more accurate. But, getting there is a matter of sticking your neck out and taking...

Initiative.

TAKE THE **INITIATIVE.**

SEIZE

YOUR OPPORTUNITY.

Will You Take the First Step?

The world isn't ending right now,
in fact, the world is yours for the taking.
So, get up, get out there, and go get it.
Take the first step
and believe in yourself even if no one else is.
Keep plugging away, set a goal, set the pace,
then take the initiative and execute.
You aren't guaranteed success
but you can't win if you don't play,
and if you don't play, you'll regret it come a time
you can't act upon it anymore.
With every second passing
time and opportunities sail away
so, get up, get out there, and go get it.
Take the first step
and believe in yourself even if no one else is.
You can search your whole life
and never find "it",
whatever "it" may be,
but that doesn't stop you now does it?

Share Your Story
About The
#Initiative_Foothold
@The_Foothold

Scan and Watch
Author Reading
and Commentary

Hop in!

The Water Sucks...

Comfort

'Trust me, I know it sucks'

Every day we are burdened with things we don't want to do. In some way shape or form. Everyday something crosses our path that makes us feel like crap. Could be your job. Could be the weather. It could be your relationship or your family. It could be your kids or your boss or even your friends. We hate confrontation with all of those things because we hate being uncomfortable. The problem is that the only way to fix any of it. Is to face that uncomfortable moment. And settle it. To step outside of our comfort zone and punch all of the obstacles that cross our paths in the face. The more we fight to go back to our comfort zone. The less you will progress in your life. The less growth you will see. The less success you will achieve. Do you want true success? Do you want a life that was worth living? Then start fighting to get comfortable outside of your comfort zone. When I'm outside working in the freezing cold, and I'm shaking because the clothes aren't protecting me any longer, and my hands are so frozen they hurt. My gloves are wet, and feet are numb. My boogers are frozen, and the wind starts to pick up again. I'm not going to break down. I'm not going to give up. I'm not going inside. I'm going to keep working. Because I don't care what this world throws in my face. I'll take it. And I'll turn it around to help me become stronger, and harder than ever before. Because I'm not a quitter. I'm a fighter. And I fight to keep myself away from the crippling feeling of...

Comfort.

BE BOLD!

TAKE THE NEXT STEP,

YOU WON'T REGRET IT.

You Know What You Need to Do

Your favorite t-shirt and jeans,
Your favorite pair of chucks,
Your favorite hat and glasses,
Your favorite sofa and ottoman
in front of your T.V and your favorite show is on.
The group of people you trust the most
And the team at work that delivers
And thrives from mutual efficiency.
The way we act within our homes
Around our family and friends in contrast to a new crowd.
The reason why we procrastinate when
we really should initiate and execute.
The way we want the best, but, shy away from testing ourselves
Because why do it today when you can do it tomorrow.
The habits we have grown so accustomed to.
They are all what makes us who we are
But how do we take the next step to evolve into someone
greater?
You take a step away from the typical
And then take It a step further because in doing so you grow.
you shed the shell and protection of your comfort zone,
You learn, adapt, and find out
who you truly are for better or for worse.
Take the step and then take it a step further.
you won't regret it.

Share Your Story
About The
#Comfort_Foothold
@The_Foothold

Scan and Watch
Author Reading
and Commentary

ACCEPT YOUR WEAKNESS, AND FIND YOUR STRENGTH.

Fear

'The real drive to adapt'

We don't get a choice. Fear haunts us every day. It may be fear of loneliness. Fear of heights. Or fear of stubbing your toe, again! What it should never be— is fear of failure. We all seem to feel that, at one point or another. It usually starts with 'what if?' And ends with 'I can't'. That is no longer an option. What if you faced your fear? You could finally see your results. The only thing you can't do, is fear what might happen if you fail. Failure will make you stronger, faster, and smarter. Fear will stop you dead in your tracks. Your brain constantly works to protect you from what is uncomfortable, and it does so with fear. But if we never face the uncomfortable by ignoring that fear, we will never find our true potential. Our priority is not only to face our fear, but to learn from it. Then, adapt to our surroundings that cause us to be fearful. It may seem like a risk, but the bigger risk is, wondering what could've been if we never faced our fears.
Leap! Adapt! Fight! Overcome!
We may not be warriors, but we must stride like one when it comes to our lives. Our mindset must change from chasing our goals, to living in our achievements. The only thing standing in our way, is...

Fear.

WILL FEAR FREEZE YOU IN YOUR TRACKS OR WILL IT BE THE MOTIVATOR THAT PROPELS YOU TO EXCEL?

Crutches and Vices

For so long you would find me
swimming in a sea of anonymity
fearfully fumbling around for fragments of
who I was and who I ought to be,
only to see that the conspiracies that I thought to be
were all my actions catching up to me.
It's amazing what you learn
when you start to fear the consequences of your own actions.
You think it's all good and fun until
getting drunk on love with a toxic lover
leads to the dozen beers you bought just today
or the shake in that Glad's sandwich baggie
you could have sworn you had more in.
Facing your fears are exponentially more difficult
when you hide behind vices and crutches to stand up to them.
So, I say it for my former self and anyone who may feel like me.
For once stand up, buck up, or shut up.

Share Your Story
About The
#Fear_Foothold
@The_Foothold

Scan and Watch
Author Reading
and Commentary

SACRIFICE

OVER

Pleasures

Risk

'Life is meant to be on the line'

Reward is something we all seek. The problem is we aren't willing to risk anything to receive it. We can't have the mentality of safety first when it comes to reaping the benefits of life. We need to live on the edge. We need to be willing to take the most dangerous routes and work through the scariest of tasks. Hiding may keep you alive but you'll always be in the bushes. Being stupid about decisions is one thing but seeing the opportunity and taking the risk to receive the reward that may become of it, that is what we actually need to seek. When we seek the hardest of tasks that is where we will find what we truly want. No one ever discovered their wildest dreams sitting on the couch. No one made their millions watching tv. No one woke up successful because they stayed at their dead-end job. No one took home the medal because they were scared to get started. No one could ever start a beautiful family and support them by lying in bed all day. The journey may be intense and seem impossible and that can scare the hell out of you. But the water is always coldest when you first get in. One toe at a time will drag out the pain. But jumping in will give you the shock of it all right away, then you adapt to the temperature. We can't fear opportunity or let it pass by because it scares us. We need to look past the pain and the suffering and take the reward we can only receive when we risk it all. Quit backing down and take a...

Risk.

DOES THE **RISK** OUTWEIGH THE REWARD?

Is It Really Worth It?

Rushing versus having patience.
You are speeding down the road 15 mph over the limit,
just to get to work when you could have woken up and left earlier.
You are not only putting yourself in danger
but you are putting those around you in danger too.
Tell me, is it really worth it?
Calculate the risk versus the reward before you advance.

Arguing and being hot-headed versus
being cool, calm, and collective.
Does the risk of confrontation
outweigh the opportunity of
establishing communication and comprehension?
Tell me, is it really worth it?
Calculate the risk versus the reward before you advance.

Being wise with your income versus
living and struggling week to week.
Does the risk of monetary issues
outweigh building for your future?
Do you want a castle made of sand,
or do you want a castle in the skies?
Tell me, is it really worth it?
Calculate the risk versus the reward before you advance.

Staying complacent versus making calculated risks.
Does the stench of stagnation
and a lifetime wasted outweigh the rewards
of living a life you end up being proud of living?
Tell me, is it really worth it?
Calculate the risk versus the reward before you advance.

You don't get a second chance.

Share Your Story
About The
#Risk_Foothold
@The_Foothold

Scan and Watch
Author Reading
and Commentary

Try
Fail
Try
Fail
CHANGE
Try
SUCCEED

Change
'What for?'

Go ahead. Try and tell me that everything in your life is perfect. I'll wait. That's what I thought. So, change it! Get away from those things that make you less of a person. find that new job that pays more and feels better to work at. get rid of all the deadbeat people in your life. The ones who will never change themselves, and always come to drag you down. Change the routine that keeps you unfit or unhealthy. Find better hobbies or entertainment that can actually help you to achieve something in your life. Nothing can actually be perfect, but nothing has to be terrible. Nothing. Treat yourself to a better life and a better you! everyone that is stuck in their ways, convince other people to become stuck as well. Change never comes without resistance. Fight it! Just take a step back and look at your life. Is it all working out? No? Then it's time for a...

Change.

Change?
I LOVE IT,
I do it Daily.

To Love is to Change

If people can't accept you for who you are
chances are they aren't as good for you
as you might have thought.
Don't settle spending your life
living for people who don't value you.
Instead, learn to value yourself.
Discover what you love and do it daily.
Make the changes now as hard as they may be.
No one else is going to do It for you.
You must love and believe in the dreams
you've always dreamt
to your hearts fullest content
even if you sever ties along the way.
What a waste it would be
to pursue love that was not your own
and what a waste it would be to love those
who are intolerant of your changes.
To love is to change as love is ever-changing–
the one true constant.

Share Your Story
About The
#Change_Foothold
@The_Foothold

Scan and Watch
Author Reading
and Commentary

This is on

You!

Excuses

'You can't? ...AAHH!'

"I can't" ... Burns-My-Brain!
Excuses mean you aren't willing to put in the work, you didn't try hard enough, or you don't care enough to achieve your goals or live up to your word. It's no one else's fault but your own. Excuses make you WEAK. Who are you trying to fool? People consciously and subconsciously frown upon any excuse no matter how small or how big it may be. An excuse means that you have not lived up to your expectations or your potential. Excuses will never fix your problems. Excuses will never actually excuse you from your situation. Take initiative.
Yes! You! Can!
You don't need excuses. If you aren't in a hospital bed right now, I don't want to hear it. You need yourself, and the strength that is inside of you, to unlock your true potential. Lead yourself to higher expectations. You don't have to prove anything to me, or anyone else for that matter. It's You that's frowning upon your actions. Surprise yourself and prove to yourself, that you are tougher than yourself, No Excuses. What separates the winners from the losers, is the winners are accountable for their actions, and the losers are always dishing out their...

Excuses.

THE MORE YOU MAKE

EXCUSES

THE MORE YOU WILL

BECOME THEM.

Worth More than an Excuse

Excuses will not cut it.
If you make excuses, you become them.
It's as simple as that.
Take a good look in the mirror and face yourself.
Look yourself dead in the eyes
and then ask yourself,
"Is an excuse all I'm worth?"
And if the answer is no,
and you know damn well that's not all you're worth,
then do yourself a favor and apply a solution even if
it's something to be fine-tuned within your own mechanics.
Make the adjustment and carry on.
You must be real with yourself
day-in and day-out, sun-up and sun-down.
Confront the parts of yourself
that have succumbed
to making excuses and face the truth.
Excuses will not cut it.
If you make excuses, you become them.
It's as simple as that.

Share Your Story
About The
#Excuses_Foothold
@The_Foothold

Scan and Watch
Author Reading
and Commentary

Can you grab me a notepad?

NOW!!! RUN!!!!!!!

Thanx.

Urgency

'Urgent! It's so urgent!'

It may not be an emergency, but urgency infused with your every move can save your life. Now a days every task just seems to be a pain in the rear. That doesn't mean we shouldn't be enthusiastic about how we do it and how fast or accurate we get it done. I'm talking about Every move. We need to do everything as if there is no more time to get it done. Something as simple as walking can prove how bad you want to succeed. Work through your day like there is no tomorrow. Like this is your last chance to get it done. No more casually strolling out to the trash can to bring out the garbage. Make it quick. Move with a swift pace. No matter where you're going. Stop spending your workdays as if you're running out the clock. Nobody has time for that mentality. It's time to get it done. If you aren't doing your tasks as quickly as you can, you're milking it. I don't care where you work or how important you think your job is. Every job is important. If you can't work the job you have like you want to be the best or prove your worth by being the most dedicated worker there, you certainly won't be any better at the job of your dreams. You won't even get the job with that attitude. You have to take every moment as if it's the cornerstone to the prosperity of your life. So put your pride aside. Work that job like it will be your last. Be the worker that everyone doesn't like because you aren't being just as lazy as the rest. Doing the jobs no one will do. Showing your value by making your every move with...

Urgency.

GO! GO! GO!

Give this life all you can give you only have one life to live.

Rise to the Occasion

"GO! GO! GO!"
Said the army officer into battle!
Okay, maybe it isn't as adrenaline filled as that command
but still, here I am saying
GO! GO! GO!
You must go achieve it, you have one life to live
don't waste it sitting around always talking but never doing.
Be urgent, rise to the occasion and get out there and live.
Fill your life with the experiences you've always imagined.
If you have goals, great!
If you have dreams, even better.
Go make one come true and then bring the next one to life.
GO! GO! GO!
You know how it goes.
Have a sense of urgency,
set a time frame, a strategic plot, and accomplish it.
Don't stop there though.
Don't stop dreaming once one has come true.
Keep raising the bar and honoring yourself.
You might not have another chance to, so
GO! GO! GO!
You know how it goes.
Maintain that sense of urgency.
You won't regret it.
When you weigh the choices, I find the answer is clear.
You live this life with urgency
knowing you are going to lose it before you know it
so, live the happiest you can now and don't regret it.
GO! GO! GO!
You know how it goes.
You don't want to regret your only chance to live.

Share Your Story
About The
#Urgency_Foothold
@The_Foothold

Scan and Watch
Author Reading
and Commentary

I WILL

NOT

GIVE UP

Perseverance

'Only a nuclear war head can stop me'

The lawn is verdant, and beautiful. Mowed 3 times a week.
Fertilized several times a year. Trimmed on the edges of the
sidewalk and where it meets the curb. Raked of the leaves in the
fall. And sprayed for weeds in the spring. But somehow. Those
weeds. They always come back. That's you, The weed. The one
they try to get rid of all the time. They think they've beaten you
down. They think they've eliminated your roots. They think
they've killed you once and for all. But you're diligent. You may be
different. You certainly stand out. But that doesn't stop you.
You're here to stay. No amount of toxicity will break you. Giving
up is not an option. You have strength. You like it here. This is
your lawn too. The grass around you may look so good and you
may be of a different color. But that doesn't distract you. That
doesn't put you down. You won't allow it. It's unacceptable. You
still plan to come back. You still plan to grow. Even when the
world doesn't like you. Doesn't matter. You aren't here to disrupt.
You aren't here to hurt anyone. You're just different. And you will
do anything in your power to break that soil,
re root yourself and thrive once more. The only thought in your
mind isn't beating discrimination it's overcoming the odds with...

Perseverance.

Do you still have the will to fight?

GOOD!

Let's get going.
We have much to achieve.

The Will to Fight

From womb to tomb
somewhere in between
where the sun shines
and the moon looms
amongst millions of stars–
This life we live will present us with suffering
and will try to break us down if we let it.
No matter what age, gender, race, or religion,
it will try and break us down.
What brings it all back together
and gives meaning to this life
against all opposition,
is finding the perseverance
stirring and festering within your soul
providing you with the will
to fight your hardest,
when the rain
pours the hardest.
For, living this life without a will to fight
is like living in hell without a fight to live.
So, get out there.
Live this life for all its worth.
Manifest the perseverance
and let the will to fight, remain.

Share Your Story
About The
#Perserverance_Foothold
@The_Foothold

Scan and Watch
Author Reading
and Commentary

Your
PERFORMANCE
Will make you
VISIBLE

Impression

'Trust me, I'm the best'

Hey! How are you? My name is….
What do you think of when you first meet someone? Not just someone you need to impress or someone you are interested in. Think about if it was someone you didn't think you would ever meet and now that you have, whatever. How do you present yourself? Tough? Sincere? The infamous 'one-up' character. Maybe you are a jokester or a know it all. Me? I'm a jerk. But how would your first impression be with that person you hope to start dating, or that, hopefully, future boss you meet at an interview? Now you're on your game, aren't you? Handing out accomplishments, skills, and great traits about yourself as if they were delicious fresh baked cookies. What if your impression wasn't a game, or a show you put on? What if it was your style? Your ability to control yourself? The confidence of a lion, but the composure of a monk. You can do this. Think before you speak and listen before you think. Absorb the personality of the other person. Observe their body language and compliment their tone with yours. Don't pretend to be someone you're not, but don't overstep boundaries with your personality or beliefs. Make sure to keep your opinions and beliefs at a level of acceptance and understanding. Don't force others to think like you, begin to think like them. Never forget who you really are. Seek what you are interested in, learn the lifestyle to live it, carry yourself with maturity, and you will always make the right…

Impression.

Even at your worst

Keep on Smiling

Its power leaves a lasting
impression

Lasting Impression

If you want happiness, manifest it.
Show the world your smile even when you are down.
Leave a lasting impression.
Define it as your own.
Continue to refine the idea of what it means to you.
Cast your mold, shape it, chisel it out,
finesse it, and focus on all the minor details
then the bigger picture will begin to take form.
Use the excess materials too–
You know, your flaws, your mistakes,
and all the chances missed
because of choices you were once too afraid act upon.
It is no longer waste,
it's repurposed to build you up from where you've been.
Rome wasn't built in a day and nor were you.
Show the world your smile even when you are down.
Leave a lasting impression.
Exhume happiness from a place of self-confidence.
Your life is the mural of your design.
Cast your mold, shape it, chisel it out,
finesse it, and cherish your greatest achievements–
Let the power of your smile
leave a lasting impression on the world.

Share Your Story
About The
#Impression_Foothold
@The_Foothold

Scan and Watch
Author Reading
and Commentary

Your

SURROUNDINGS

Are Your

OPPORTUNITIES

Awareness

'Open Your Eyes'

Our self-awareness is so important for us to take a hold of. Realizing that we have control over our body and mind at any given moment. Pretending that we don't is irresponsible. I constantly made excuses for my thoughts or actions. Telling myself it was just who I was. That I couldn't change it or make it better. I just assumed I would have to cope with these feelings. I am who I am. Living with the pain. Ignore the health problems and move on. Taking my inner being for granted has blocked me from completing tasks, wanting to do the right thing, and staying healthy. It was only once I finally gave it a chance that my eyes were opened. Our minds are like sponges. If we aren't aware of how to use it. We never add water. It stays dry, hard, and worthless. We need to add water. Allow it to absorb everything. Then add soap. So we can clean out the dirt in our lives. Always rinse it out and start fresh. Keeping our sponge from becoming rancid. I clear my thoughts every night. Erase the other thoughts my mind consistently holds on to. Leaving a clean slate for another day. A new day. A Fresh thought. A clear and open mind. Waiting to absorb that new material. Prepared to take on those hidden opportunities. Storing energy to attempt new endeavors I previously wouldn't have even tried to do. I began to notice more of my surroundings. Find better shoes to walk in. Seeking clearer thoughts. Thriving in the new life I have created with, one hundred percent, self-...

Awareness.

Be

AWARE

of your

IMPACT

The Nutrients

If there is a lesson to be taught
see to it that it is taught correctly.
Be aware of the impact you have on those around you.
It isn't always about your image.
Give gifts to the open minds
that are willing to absorb knowledge
like the roots of trees absorbing rainfall.
Feed those around you the nutrients
you once took in for your own growth.
Be aware of your impact and spread your knowledge.
Teach without bias.
Teach without anger.
Teach without arrogance.
Teach with compassion.
Teach with patience.
Teach with understanding.
It is not belittling.
It is not condescension.
It is leading.
It is making one aware while being self-aware.
Be aware of the impact you have on those around you.

Share Your Story
About The
#Awareness_Foothold
@The_Foothold

Scan and Watch
Author Reading
and Commentary

NEVER
LET YOURSELF
DOWN

Consistency

'You always do that!'

Be a dependable person. There are things we look at in people that we don't even realize. Whether they always show up, and on time, they're always prepared for the situation, or even always know a lot about something specific. That constant reminder is from consistent actions. You need to be that person. Nothing catches you by surprise. You're ready and able. Don't leave people worrying about whether you're going to come through or not. They know you're someone of their word. Say what you mean and mean what you say. The task may vary, or the situations may be specific, but that's why they called YOU! The value others see in you will consistently rise, even if you aren't the best. Even more importantly than others, you'll see more value in yourself. Prioritize your routine. Be dependent on yourself. Never let yourself down. Substantial growth is inevitable when you gain ground on your...

Consistency.

If AnYtHiNg, Be
CoNsIsTeNt
To WhO yOu ArE
aNd To wHo yOu
ArE bEcOmInG.

CoNsIsTeNcY

Like the letters of the title
stay CoNsIsTeNt to who you are
and to who you are becoming even if
it differs from the next person.
Gather your mind to find clear and refined thoughts
that lead you toward CoNsIsTeNt actions.
Stay CoNsIsTeNt to who you are
and to who you are becoming even if
it differs from the next person.
Let your uniqueness define you.
If you spread yourself too thin
by worrying about outside commentary,
you'll begin to lose sight of your CoNsIsTeNcY
and question your own purpose.
Spread your wings and fly away from the nonsensical.
Stay CoNsIsTeNt to that.
Define yourself by being you, unapologetically.

Be CoNsIsTeNt.

Share Your Story
About The
#Consistency_Foothold
@The_Foothold

Scan and Watch
Author Reading
and Commentary

Embrace it.

Use it.

LIVE BY IT!

Criticism

'OooO I needed this!'

If there is one thing I can think of right off the bat when it comes to criticism. It's how easy it is to give it away and how shamefully difficult it is to receive it. But there is something to be said for someone who takes it and puts it to work. We all need to be confident and determined. We need to believe in ourselves, our work, and our ideas. That doesn't mean we can't accept criticism and make our lives better. I tend to be a thoroughly blunt person once I get to know someone. It's a flaw that I have, but oddly its' my way of showing you affection. I can't help it. I simply want you to do better. I, however, enjoy being criticized. It may hurt at first and I may not agree. I may even argue with you, but I take it into consideration before my pride just throws it away. You can never see life from every perspective. That's where our critics come in handy. Let them say what they want. They may not always be correct. They may not always have the right path in mind for you. But it's something to consider if you hadn't already. Never throw criticism away. It's the downfall of us all. Even If you legitimately have researched the path suggested or gone down it already. Maybe you missed something or maybe you're just afraid. Maybe something subconsciously just tells you, "No". But knowing in your mind that someone may see something you don't, and accepting it, can lead to what may be your biggest breakthrough. Don't take it for granted. Be sure to keep people in your circle who have the same goals or have achieved your goals to keep the criticism relevant. And don't get confused, 'Nay Sayers' can change your mind because they just couldn't do something themselves. That's not the criticism you're looking for. Be sure that it is constructive. Never be close-minded, leaving yourself open to the thoughts of those who are successful and offer you the gift of...

Criticism.

IF YOU DISH IT OUT YOU BETTER BE WILLING TO EAT IT.

Give and Take

If you can't take it, don't dish it out.
Find another way to say it
or just keep your comments to yourself.
Think before you speak and before you act,
think about how the recipient might react.
Every action has a reaction.
I've learned that when receiving it
you can't take it personal.
There is an art to it.
Some individuals take it differently.
Some in stride and some take it more to heart.
You must distinguish the correct way to communicate
or else you might be on the receiving end of
a defense mechanism instead of something productive.
This applies to your inner dialogue as well.
Sometimes we're so hard on ourselves,
It's counterproductive.
We have such high standards
We forget we are only human.
Can we accept the hardest truths about ourselves
as well as those of another person?
It's both taken and given.
If you decide you are going to dish it out
you better be willing to eat it.
You either harness it or let it destroy you.
How will you handle criticism?

Share Your Story
About The
#Criticism_Foothold
@The_Foothold

Scan and Watch
Author Reading
and Commentary

What are you DOING ? !

Priorities

'No! I don't want to watch tv!'

Where is your spare time being spent? I'm well aware that we all have to work for a living. I'm also well aware of what exhaustion feels like after it. I'm, honestly, curious how many of you are doing something productive with your lives after work. Are you hitting the gym? Are you going to school? Are you working a side hustle? Do you even have a hobby? There's no time to waste in this precious life we live. Don't give me that, 'I just want to relax', nonsense. We all want to lay down, do nothing, and still get by in life. Especially me! But just in case you were wondering, that isn't going to happen! Not without prioritizing your life around hard work and dedication. Pushing toward that exact thing as your life goal. If you want to prioritize relaxing and watching tv, go ahead. I hope that works out for you. As for me, spear heading my problems, seeking out the hard tasks, and working my butt off, are my only...

Priorities.

PRIORITIZE YOURSELF

OVER WHAT DRAGS
YOU
DOWN.

Be You, For You

In search of myself and I mean my true inner self
I realized that I need to be me, for me.
Prioritizing myself above
what tries to drag me down and keep me there.
Those that accept me I gladly stand tall beside
and as for those who oppose me
weighing down on me like gravity
I will gladly leave in hindsight.
These keen eyes are homed in on my dreams
and are aware of those with intentions aimed to demean.
I won't become someone for anyone.
The same goes for you too,
the reader, the poet, the writer,
or whoever you chalk yourself up to be.
Be you, for you.
Don't become someone for anyone.
Self-reliance and self-prioritization
are the ultimate weapons of defiance
against those who want you to become someone for no one.
I repeat, don't become someone for anyone.
Be you, for you.
Prioritize yourself above what drags you down.

Share Your Story
About The
#Priorities_Foothold
@The_Foothold

Scan and Watch
Author Reading
and Commentary

DON'T FORGET YOUR HEAD

Preparation

'What if your only chance is now?'

Don't be late. For goodness' sake, Don't Be Late!
Are you 5 steps ahead? 10 steps ahead!?! Good.
You should be. The only thing that's stopping you from succeeding when you are prepared, is the opportunity. When it comes, you'd better be breaking your ankles turning away from everything. If you're not, then it's no wonder you haven't succeeded. You should be prepared for anything. Something as small as having an extra pen in your pocket just in case your boss is walking by and needs to look good, but doesn't have one, and you do. You give it to them, on the spot before they even ask!! Terrible example, but you get the idea. Preparation can't be taken for granted. And it doesn't only mean materialistic preparation either. Mental preparation is something that will break the ground before you. Think of how great you were when you first met that special someone. You were ready, early, cleaned up, and smiling. You were ready to talk about all your great achievements in life, even if there hadn't been any, Yet. But if you lose that, and you aren't prepared at all times to be that person, simply by being that person every day, you'll fall off. You'll never keep growing. You'll never keep that special someone. You'll be a phony. You could never create that business or impress that new big client you are trying so hard to work with. You aren't ready. You must be that person who never lets anyone down. That person everyone can count on. They know you will never forget. They know you always have what you need, and more importantly you always have what it takes. You strive to never underestimate your tasks, and your performance is always impeccable. The only reason you can do this so affectively, so efficiently, and so prominently, is because you had turned your realty into a lifestyle of...

Preparation.

BE PREPARED TO *Change*.
IT'S INEVITABLE.

Your Entire Approach

Will you be prepared to change?
I ask because to grow mentally, physically, and emotionally
You're going to have to adjust your entire approach.
At any moment you must be prepared
to face the best or worst of the day you are facing.
Some days are going to be awful
from the time your alarm goes off,
up until you are ready to go to bed again,
and hell, you might find your troubles
linger into your next night's sleep as well.
When you face the long nights of over thinking
while your head space is a thunderstorm at sea,
will you be mentally prepared
to sail yourself back to the harbor again?
When you look at yourself in the mirror and think
I could love myself a little bit more
by working out or making better habits
will you be physically prepared
to adjust to a new routine?
The next time someone is offensive,
will you react brashly
or will you be emotionally prepared
to detach yourself from that negativity
in order to respond in a respectful manner?
Your entire approach must change.
Will you be prepared to change your entire approach?

Share Your Story
About The
#Preparation_Foothold
@The_Foothold

Scan and Watch
Author Reading
and Commentary

PERFECT is GOOD ENOUGH

Meticulous

'You see that?'

"It's the little things", they always say. Why is that? Because its true! The little things that piss you off. The little things that get you fired. The little things that can make your significant other feel like they can't stand you anymore. Where is the line in the sand? Nowhere! It's never enough. But, an eye for detail can be a golden trait. Pay close attention to fine details. Remember the tiny facts and features. Do what no one would expect you to do. Look deeper than the surface. Then do it and do it right the first time. Open your eyes, be aware of your surroundings. Never compromise for less than perfect. Your hard work will portray the person you are to the people you should. Some people who are not perfectionists will hate this! Let them hate it. Strive for total perfection with every performance. Seek and find the things no one else can even see or think of. No one ever lost their way by being...

Meticulous.

1st *Part* – KNOW YOUR PATH.

2nd *Part* – BE METICULOUS.

3rd *Part* – EXECUTE.

Three Darts

Before your first throw,
think, take a breath, and be meticulous.
Focus on where you want to be.
Your first throw hits and you've made your mark.
As for the second throw,
think, take a breath, and be meticulous.
It's everything in between that counts
and you only have so many chances.
Don't hit the triple-one while aiming for the triple-twenty.
As for your third throw,
It's do or die,
you know how it goes.
It's just like playing Cricket–
three marks and you're closed out
better make them count.

Share Your Story
About The
#Meticulous_Foothold
@The_Foothold

Scan and Watch
Author Reading
and Commentary

Quit!

Wasting!

Moves!

Efficiency
'Every Footstep Counts'

There is a place in our heads where we think of this word and appliances come to mind. If you work in a trade maybe your machinery, fixtures, or heating systems. If you are into cars maybe it's the gas mileage or how far an electric car can drive before it needs to be charged. Honestly, humans are no different. Depending on how we are treated, we last much longer. We work harder. We do a better job. The problem is we try to determine our efficiency by looking at how others treat us. That isn't how we work. It's how we treat ourselves, our bodies, and our minds. How we eat and sleep. Technically, we can all be considered machines. Without the proper maintenance or proper use, we deteriorate and become worthless. Eventually, we end up replaced. What if we found those problems before we became inefficient? What if we constantly looked for those things and proactively worked on them before they beat us down? We all know what needs to be done to make ourselves better, we just don't do it. But with machinery and technology taking over our world as we know it, we as humans need to start to be more efficient than ever. We need our bodies to last longer. We need our brains to work harder and faster. We need to consistently push ourselves to the limits every day, working towards being as efficient as possible. I'm not just talking about at your day job either. I mean everything! The dishes. The laundry. Mowing the lawn. Your morning routine. We need to focus on our diets and our education most importantly! Even though humans will always be the fuel to our existence, we cannot take for granted how important it is to structure our life to be one of...

Efficiency.

Be so efficient
that it becomes influential.

SET THE EXAMPLE.

Influential Efficiency

If you are genuinely committed to making a change
you must approach the hardships of life
with strides toward an efficient solution.
You haven't any time to squander.
You should know by now that life is far too short.
Make a list and tackle your hardships head on
and one by one they will prepare you for the next round.
Life is nothing short of persistent.
Find a way to keep striving toward that efficiency,
because giving up isn't a productive solution.
In fact, it's just an excuse.
It's an excuse that sets an awful example.
Instead, take a stand and spread a positive attitude.
In the face of hardship and suffering
show the people around you how to stand up for themselves
in hopes that they can spread influential efficiency.
Just imagine the consistent examples of
self-efficient solution seeking attitudes
having the potential to influence a countless number of people.
Before you know it,
you have created a mutual-minded network
of combined effort and efficiency.
A unit of individuals that are set to make a change.

Share Your Story
About The
#Efficiency_Foothold
@The_Foothold

Scan and Watch
Author Reading
and Commentary

THE
PATH
LESS TRAVELLED
IS A

BEAUTIFUL

BUMPY ROAD

Direction
O' Lighthouse

Show me the way!
Majestic beams trail the waves,
submerged in inspiration.

O' Lighthouse

Show me the way!
Countless rejections in my days,
soaked in motivation.

O' Lighthouse

Show me the way!
Painful loss from time we waste,
saturated in admiration.

O' Lighthouse

I've found the way!
Tears of joy,
washed in exaltation.

O' Lighthouse

My lack of direction

redirected me to

the greateast truths.

Without Direction

How sweet joy is
when sorrow is far too bitter,
and how sweet pleasure is
when pain is overpowering.

How sweet the truth is
when all your ears have heard are lies,
and how sweet the heat of love is
when your heart has been absent from its presence.

How sweet the quench of thirst is
when your tongue begs for water,
and how sweet the taste of food is
when you've been starved of nourishment.

How sweet the heat of an open flame is
when your hands have gone stiff and cold,
and how sweet are the gusts of wind
when you're lost at sea without direction.

Share Your Story
About The
#Direction_Foothold
@The_Foothold

Scan and Watch
Author Reading
and Commentary

Get Back Up
AND SWING

Resilience

'Bounce back hard!'

Obstacles cross our path every day, but that's no reason to bring everything to a screeching halt. We have goals to meet. We have dreams to achieve. Our mistakes are merely the steppingstones on our path to success. Difficulties are the pebbles between these stones. Tragedy is the wind that causes resistance. We need these things. We look for these things. We push back against these things. We take these steps even though they may be uncomfortable. We learn from them no matter how miniscule or substantial the lesson may be. In order to break ground on new accomplishments and smash our competition, we need the knowledge from our experiences that could have never been found if we were too scared to fail. The definition of the person we want to become, will begin to unfold when we start to forcefully test our own...

Resilience.

RESILIENCE IS AN ART FOR THE STOUT-HEARTED, NOT FOR THE FAINT OF HEART.

The Mantra of Resilience

When scaling a mountain as vast as life itself
there isn't any time to second guess,
nor is there any room for cracking under pressure.
This is the foothold to our success.
With our heels dug in,
our actions show the world how we feel.
To possess enough inner strength,
to press on and bounce back,
even when the trail gets rugged.
This is the foothold to our success.
With our heels dug in,
our actions show the world how we deal.
To have enough heart to recover,
to have an instinctual prowess powering on,
and understanding that the next step
is before you, not behind you.
This is the foothold to our success.
With our heels dug in,
our actions show the world two wills
that must be revealed.

Share Your Story
About The
#Resilience_Foothold
@The_Foothold

Scan and Watch
Author Reading
and Commentary

THE DAY BEFORE YESTERDAY IS THE NEW TODAY'S TOMMORRROW

Procrastination

'I don't feel good, I'll just do it...'

STOP! Forget what you're feeling, stop what you're doing, get off your behind, and get it done! Stop waiting to get those important or not so important things done. There will never be a better day or a better time. Now is the answer. The more you do now, the less you have to do later. Don't procrastinate things that annoy or irritate you. They will just do the same exact thing the next time you have to do it. Simply, get up, take initiative, and do what you need to do! The greatest people on this earth didn't become great by saying "well, we can just do it tomorrow,". NO! They didn't stop until they had achieved the things they needed to achieve. Don't let your life pass you by because you're tired or not feeling up to the task. Sick? Tired? Dying? Not an excuse! You don't have the time to waste, no one does. Your hopes, your dreams, your life — will all be destroyed if you constantly resort to...

Procrastination.

JUST BECAUSE YOU PUSH IT OFF DOESN'T MEAN THE CLOCK STOPS TICKING.

Procrastination

It's one of those tasks I knew I needed to do.
But why do it today?
I can just take tomorrow for granted and wait it out!
It has been on my mind for weeks and I'm approaching the deadline
like a sprinter headed toward the finish line.
Anxiety riddles my mind.
What am I going to do!?
I should have just done it shortly after I got it.
I do this every time, now I'm here again,
and I'm sure you've been there too.
It's one of those tasks I knew I needed to do.
But why do it today?
I can just take tomorrow for granted and wait it out!
You know how it goes,
we tell ourselves we will be prompt,
we will work out our problems,
we will eliminate our bad habits,
and open that business you keep telling your friends about.
I told you, it's one of those tasks I knew I needed to do.
But why do it today?
I can just take tomorrow for granted and wait it out!
It's the human paralysis–
we are constantly thinking thoughts,
continuously speaking of them,
yet have no plan of action.
That's what you should be terrified of.
You are carrying on like a paved road leading to nowhere,
until that defining moment—
when you are face to face with the real you.
The you, you know you need to be.

Share Your Story
About The
#Procrastination_Foothold
@The_Foothold

Scan and Watch
Author Reading
and Commentary

Bring Back
The

HONOR

System

Humility

'Who do you think you are?'

Do you glorify yourself? Do you seek credit for your every action? Do you really deserve it? What do you deserve? The truth is, we all seek credit for the things we do, but is it worth it? Will it actually make a difference in your life today? Will it make you a better person? Will it make you a real company-loyal person? Probably not. The glory is never yours. It isn't something we deserve. Our lives should never be driven by glory. It should be driven by our self-worth, not self-loathing. We don't need others to be jealous of us. We only need to seek the greater good, the best for our environment, and the best for the ones who surround us. We must work to make a difference in the places we go. Not for our own good, but for everyone. Entitlement isn't the answer to getting what we want. We earn exactly what we truly deserve. The more you seek what you feel is right, the further it gets away from us. Take others into consideration. Especially when you don't know who they are and may never meet them. Whether you leave this world known or not isn't important. It's how you leave the world behind you that is important. Forget what you think you're entitled to and stay humble. Your true worth is only valued by your true...

Humility.

BE HUMBLE.
Try modesty mixed with honesty.

The Shoe Could Be on the Other Foot

You can be proud of how far you've come,
but don't be arrogant.
It flaws your character,
and all of the time you spent pounding your chest,
is just a façade, sheltering the shallow person inside.
I mean, whoever liked a showoff anyway?
Instead, be humble.
Try modesty mixed with honesty.
The shoe could be on the other foot.
Focus on your goals, dreams, and aspirations,
unafraid of letting your guard down.
Know when to ask for and accept a pair of helping hands.
Manage yourself and learn from the mistakes
you are constantly making along the way.
It's the only way to comprehend, let alone understand.
When you see others struggling to regain their balance,
holding onto whatever little pride they have left,
understand before you look down on them,
that easily could've been you—
So instead, be humble.
Try modesty mixed with honesty.
The shoe could be on the other foot.

Share Your Story
About The
#Humility_Foothold
@The_Foothold

Scan and Watch
Author Reading
and Commentary

In the

Waiting

There is an

Abundance of

TIME

Patience

'How bad do you want it?'

Well... too bad! Wait. Nothing happens overnight. We all know this. Yet we constantly try to search for ways to receive that instant gratification. Success is surely not instant. It takes time, it takes obsession, it takes patience, and passion. Those with success put their blood, sweat, and tears into it. It took huge risks to achieve it. They waited forever for that promotion. For their idea to be heard of. For their business to take off. While constantly being told it wasn't possible and that they were crazy. And not to mention receiving rejection after rejection. They spent countless hours, days, even years of their lives to create the life they have today. Giving up probably came to mind a hundred times over, yet they were patient with their failures. They were patient with the number of meticulous actions they took to finally make it. It will come. Just visualize the success, put in the work every single day, and don't ever quit. Then, most importantly, practice...

Patience.

*You know what you need to do
so don't rush it.*

HAVE PATIENCE.

Have Patience

Walk through life,
don't run through it.
If you need to run,
do it in moderation.
Efficiency isn't rushed.
It's in the synchronicity all around us.
You don't want to miss crucial details
because you ran by.
Take the time to enjoy the view—
You might learn something you never knew.
The tortoise makes its way eventually
and chances are once it does,
it shares similar satisfaction to the hare.
Truth is, if you work hard toward your goal
the sense of accomplishment is relative.

Share Your Story
About The
#Patience_Foothold
@The_Foothold

Scan and Watch
Author Reading
and Commentary

Lending a *Hand* Is Better than Receiving a *FOOT*

Support

'We all need Nobody, to lean on.'

Is there something you wish that you knew? Is there somewhere that you want your life to be? Get out there and figure it out on your own. Don't sit around waiting for other people to hand you that golden egg that will give you everything you need. What's stopping you from figuring it out? Failure? Big whoop. Failure is the only thing that's going to teach you. If you're getting by today with someone else's income, someone else's roof over your head, someone else's vehicle bringing you to work, or someone else's food going into your mouth. Then you need to start thinking about how you're going to support yourself. Get out there and start new things on your own. Troubleshoot your own life. Fail as much as you can. Work your way up to a point where you can give somebody else your...

Support.

KEEP MOVING FOWARD,
EVERY ACTION
SUPPORTS THE NEXT ONE.

Structure

Support one another,
like the Golden Gate Bridge—
Even when the wind is fierce
you bend but don't break,
for you know what is at stake.

Support one another,
like the rigidity of the General Sherman's foundation—
Even when it is tested by nature,
its gigantic structure stands tall
withstanding the test of time.

Support one another,
like the Hoover Dam—
Holding back mass amounts of water,
it's under pressure,
yet remains resilient.

Support one another,
because our lives depend on it—
Our existence thrives
off of how we prosper as a whole.
Every action supports the next.

Share Your Story
About The
#Support_Foothold
@The_Foothold

Scan and Watch
Author Reading
and Commentary

THE ONLY THING YOU SHOULD FEEL IS

DETERMINATION

Emotion

'Quit over exaggerating!'

Everyone's emotions are off the charts! Maybe there would be less happiness without it, but the benefits outweigh the downfalls. People would be healthier, stronger, and altogether more efficient. You wouldn't feel sad or upset, angry or unhappy, there would only be more progress. No crime, no harassment, and less failure. No love, but also, no hate. Even the things people love about emotion cause problems. Racism is driven by emotion. Politics have gone from policies and reforms to emotions! Emotion has divided us all! But eliminating emotion isn't possible. Therefore, we need to stop feeling so much. Stop caring about the things that don't matter. Focus on the things that do. Think logically, not emotionally. Use our emotions to drive us to be the best we can be. Instead of thinking with emotion, we need to start working with...

Emotion.

THE TIME HAS COME
FOR YOU TO RESOLVE YOUR
EMOTIONS
AND GO ALL IN.

Holding You Back

The clusters of negative emotions
holding you back are painful, aren't they?
They're like a lingering headache behind your eyes.
Well, it's time to resolve them.
Accept the hand you've been dealt
and find new ways to play your cards,
even if the deck is stacked against you.
Go all in!
You've been infused with
cumbersome anger
for far too long.
Release it, you don't need it.
You've been hit with the fury of anxiety.
Take a breath, slow down, refocus your wit,
and lift the deadweight of depression
crushing your collarbones.
It's time to resolve this.
It's only holding you back.
Robbing you of surpassing your greatest potential.
Find ways to motivate and inspire yourself.
Set goals and achieve them at your pace,
or find yourself digging your own grave daily.

Share Your Story
About The
#Emotion_Foothold
@The_Foothold

Scan and Watch
Author Reading
and Commentary

YOU MUST PROTECT YOURSELF FROM YOURSELF

Discipline

'This is on you'

Setting goals is one thing, achieving those goals is another. If there's one thing in this world that will get you to achieve those goals, it's discipline. The consistent actions and hard decisions will create an environment that compliments those goals. Your dreams alone won't be enough. It's your state of mind, continually making the decisions that keep you on track. What you choose today will affect your tomorrow. You need to do it. You need to hold yourself to a standard that allows nothing but your success. Hard work is one thing, persistence is another. If you work hard for one day but don't the next, failure will be your end game. Discipline will keep you consistent and productive. Your heart can't triumph over your mind. You need to say with your mouth, 'I need to do this, and I will', even when you don't want to and especially when you can't! Discipline yourself and seek the hard way out. Discipline yourself and seek the hard tasks first! The only way to get to where you want to go, is to construct your path around…

Discipline.

MAINTAIN DISCIPLINE

AND YOUR HARD WORK

WILL TAKE SHAPE.

I've

To rid the pain of this life,
I've let my mind
become lost
in countless poems.
I've let my soul soar
through several stories,
I've let them tap into my being.
I've watched my essence drip away,
drop
by
drop
like sap
from a maple tree.
Page by page,
chapter by chapter,
I've let my words become my master.

Share Your Story
About The
#Discipline_Foothold
@The_Foothold

Scan and Watch
Author Reading
and Commentary

IF YOU CAN

RELaX

WITHOUT HAVING IT,

YOU DON'T WANT IT!

Desire

'Visualize your future'

Can you see it? Your dream? How bad do you want it? So bad that it hurts? That's not enough! You need to want it more! You need to see it when you close your eyes! Believe that it will happen! Forget all of the things that point the other way. Everybody wants something, and they want it bad. You need to want it more than them. You need to work harder than them. The only way you'll be able to do this, is to focus. This isn't just hope. It isn't about pride. It's about pushing yourself beyond the likes of you. Don't focus on talk, focus on the action. Pain must drive you. Failure must inspire you. Criticism must derive from you. It isn't something that you will find, you must obtain it. Seek your opportunities and take them by surprise. You must always be willing and ready to put in that work no one else is ready and willing to do. Take this lightly, and someone else will steal your dream from beneath you. A win isn't given, it's acquired by the one who was driven, calloused with defeat, and fueled by...

Desire.

TO STOKE THE FLAMES
OF YOUR DESIRE
YOU HAVE TO LEAVE YOUR COMFORT
ZONE IN ASHES.

Something More

I've resided inside the confines of conformity
for what seems like an eternity.
It's time for me to wake up and erupt into something more
than this monotony my life has become.
There has to be something more to me.
There has to be something more to achieve.
There has to be something more to believe.
There has to be something more to inspire.
If I adopt a new way of thinking,
use the will inside of me and act upon it,
then repeat what acted in my benefit,
it will translate my inner visions to the world.
To stoke the flames of your desires
you have to leave your comfort zone in ashes.
There has to be something more.
There has to be.
These dreams aren't going to chase themselves.

Share Your Story
About The
#Desire_Foothold
@The_Foothold

Scan and Watch
Author Reading
and Commentary

Who do you

NEED

To be?

Integrity

'Nothing should compromise your soul'

Who are you when no one is looking? What describes you? Is there a definition in the dictionary that should be your name? If not, let this word be it. Don't end up like everyone else. Live on good morals. Even bad people like a person with the right attitude. You don't need to act in charity, in fact, don't. It's bigger than that. Just think of everyone you see as a good friend or family member. Think of others before every action. If everyone could get their morals together while in public places, less people would argue. Less people would fight. Less people would shoot! More people would work harder and give a helping hand. Instead, we've become selfish and vigorous. When one person does this, everyone gets the idea that they can act the same way. This needs to stop. If we can't be true to ourselves, how can we prove ourselves to other people. What you do behind closed doors will describe who you really are. It's time to start living an admirable life. A life of true...

Integrity.

WHEN VALUES AND ACTIONS
BECOME PARALLEL
IS WHEN INTEGRITY IS
CONCEIVED.

Integrity

Spread the positivity in life,
even if no one is around to watch
or pat you on the back for doing so.
It could be something as simple as being uplifting and motivated.
You have the strength to inspire with your actions.
It can come in the form of being a good listener
with a sturdy shoulder to lean on.
It could even start by greeting a stranger
with eye contact, a genuine smile, and a
"Hi, how are you doing today?",
instead of darting your eyes elsewhere.
Be honest with yourself and those around you.
Before you judge someone,
know that just because some individuals do awful things,
it doesn't mean everyone else shares that similarity.
Trust, and have faith that strong morals will hold precedence.
Spread the positivity in life,
even if no one is around to watch
or pat you on the back for doing so.
We can do this together and it starts
by taking that initial notion of positivity
and letting it become the root of what defines you.
If violence and hatred beget hate,
then let the positivity in your life beget more positivity.
Do yourself and your neighbor this favor—
Bring positivity to this life
without expectations of something in return
other than knowing you bred integrity.

Share Your Story
About The
#Integrity_Foothold
@The_Foothold

Scan and Watch
Author Reading
and Commentary

You are Better than this.

Expectation

'What did you expect?'

When you expect things to happen, you'll always be disappointed. When you expect your financial situation to fix itself. When you expect your dreams to come true without having a plan. When you expect your moment to come, and you never actually put in the effort. It leaves you with exactly what you had all along, expectations. Expectations have no value, only hard work does. No one ever became the next best business entrepreneur or world class athlete because they expected it to happen to them. They put the skin into the game that no one else would, expected nothing, and worked for everything! That mindset is what creates the real character in a person and, ultimately, leading to success. When the most necessary expectations can't be met, don't make yourself miserable. Use it as fuel and push yourself even harder. Never give up, otherwise you'll never live up to your own...

Expectations.

*Excpect more of yourself
rather than expect more
from the world around you
it owes you nothing.*

Expectation

What did you expect?
If all you're going to give is 25% of your best efforts
and your best efforts top out at 50%,
you do the math—
Can you really have an expectation
of anything more than failure?
If no one has said anything yet,
WAKE UP!
The world owes you nothing!
You won't make worth of this life
sitting around twiddling your thumbs.
If you want something worth having, then work for it.
I can't stress it enough.
By no means will it be easy.
Hell, it might be the hardest thing
that you've ever done in your entire life.
You still must try.
If you're going to expect anything,
expect to bring the best version of you
for as long as you live.
The world owes you nothing!
You exist here on this Earth, healthy and striving,
which is the greatest gift you could receive.
If no one has said anything yet,
WAKE UP!
The world owes you nothing!

Share Your Story
About The
#Expectation_Foothold
@The_Foothold

Scan and Watch
Author Reading
and Commentary

Whatever is going on, I'm sure that it's

YOU!

Denial

'You are your own problem'

No, it wasn't the economy. Nope, it wasn't the market. No way, it definitely wasn't the competition. Well...maybe it was, but only because they faced the facts and dealt with their problems as if it was their fault. Blaming everything except for yourself, is denial. It's denying the fact that you just weren't ready. You just weren't prepared to succeed. You didn't set yourself up for success to begin with. You just expected it to go exactly how you wanted it to, and...it didn't. Surprise! There's always the 'what if's' and the 'if only's'. This time, there needs to be the 'I should have'! The more you tell yourself that it's the fault of something or someone else, the more you will depend on that excuse. Waiting for what could've been if only that thing didn't screw you. The reality is. YOU, SCREWED YOU. Take responsibility for everything that isn't going the way you had hoped. Soon, what should've been, will be. Or you can spend the rest of your life in...

Denial.

Don't deny your

MISTAKES

learn from them.

Owning Up

If you're wrong, you're wrong.
If you make a mistake, you made a mistake.
Making excuses will leave you in denial.
Accept when you are wrong
and if you have a swan song to sing
go down to the nearest lake and sing it to the birds
because no one has time for your crap, trust me.
Don't deny your mistakes,
stand by them and learn from them,
even when it's painful.
I've been trapped in that cage,
blind-folded by denial and meaningless pride.
I looked over the fact that being so adamant
made me close-minded.
I was so sure I was right,
so consumed by pride.
I denied any chance of being wrong.
Yet now within that acknowledgement
I set myself free.
Do yourself a favor,
let yourself be free—
Free of meaningless pride, free of denial,
and be you through and through.
Don't deny your mistakes,
stand by them and learn from them,
even when it's painful.

Share Your Story
About The
#Denial_Foothold
@The_Foothold

Scan and Watch
Author Reading
and Commentary

SET YOURSELF FREE

Forgiveness

'You'll carry the burden, not them'

The hardest thing for a human being to do, is to forgive another. I love when hard things cross my path. I accept the challenge. The grudges make us fight while reminding us of where we came from. I use them as fuel, but I will no longer hold it against another. I hold it to myself. I keep it as a scar. I grow confident with who I am because of the downfall. It isn't their fault any longer. It's now mine. Do I forgive myself? I must! My energy is no longer worth the unnecessary burden. You might say it can't be forgiven. You're wrong. You might've let it happen, or maybe you didn't have a choice. But right here, right now, you do have a choice. A choice that can either hold you back forever or set you free. Will you let this hardship determine your fate? Will you allow this strain to tear you down further? No. This isn't about those difficulties any longer. This is about growth. This is about fulfillment. This is about the life you can finally start to love when you release those demons. Inner growth begins with...

Forgiveness.

Forgiveness begins within

What Was, Is All It Will Be

I had to fall to rock bottom
to learn how to climb back to the top of the rock.
When I was at my worst,
I had no one to blame but myself
if I didn't fight for my own existence.
I've forgiven myself
but haven't forgotten.
I had to see loved ones dwindle away to understand
my youth didn't grant me invincibility.
The pain of loss was devastating,
but the world owes me nothing.
I was granted the gift of life.
I've forgiven myself
but haven't forgotten
how these experiences matured me emotionally.
I had to make mistakes
and survive broken heartedness,
to know how to accept what was, is all it will be.
To see that the forgiveness I've needed all along
begins within.

Share Your Story
About The
#Forgiveness_Foothold
@The_Foothold

Scan and Watch
Author Reading
and Commentary

WHEN I'M IN IT
I'M IN IT

Commitment

'The Handshake'

Posture proves your worth.

Unbroken eye contact.

Forward assertion.

No weakness in gesture.

Beckoning thumbs interlock cleanly.

Strong, firm, tightening grip.

Less than a stubborn jar.

Humble with your confident demeanor.

Facial expression proving honesty.

Stepping backward.

An opportunistic agreement.

Your future is on the line.

Committed.

FIND WHAT YOU LOVE AND STAY COMMITTED.

The Machinist

19 years ago, I was 10 years old and on the verge of graduating from Bucks Hill Elementary School. I was convinced that I would be a Machinist just like my older brother Chris. When we had to write what we wanted to be when we were older in the yearbook, I simply put "Machinist", amongst all the other student's occupation selections of CIA agents, actors, lawyers, designers, and teachers. I genuinely hope that every one of my fellow 2002 classmates stayed committed to their dreams. I know I did. It might not hold much merit on its own, just saying I became a machinist, but I stayed committed to a dream I had since elementary school. I specifically wanted to attend the trade school W.F Kaynor Technical Highschool to pursue it. I was ecstatic when I received my acceptance letter. By the time my junior year rolled around I turned 16 and was able to go out on the Connecticut Worked Based Learning Program. I was a pre-apprentice at Edward Segal Incorporated. Once I graduated, the company decided to hire me. I officially became a legitimate tool making apprentice. Today, I'm a licensed CNC Machinist Journeyman, with potential to continue to shape my manufacturing career. I was able to manifest my own destiny. This simple dream of mine as a child is now 19 years in the making and I absolutely love what I do. I found what I loved and remained committed to it. That there, is the silver lining of this all. I remained committed to what I love and that has given me fulfillment. I will keep dreaming and keep fulfilling my dreams. I will remain…

Committed.

Share Your Story
About The
#Commitment_Foothold
@The_Foothold

Scan and Watch
Author Reading
and Commentary

TRY ME!

Confidence

'You know it can be.'

If you don't believe in yourself, progress will be impossible. When you're confident in yourself, you get that drive that many people lack. It's the drive to try again even when you fail. To try and win even when you always lose. No matter who you are, there's confidence in you. You can do something and you're good at it. Many of us like to tell others that we are better than them. That's not confidence. Confidence will keep the things they say from stopping you. Find that one thing you love to do and be confident in yourself. Train your subconscious to create a more positive outlook and a more confident perspective. This is the way to fight through that wall. If you want something, you need to take it. And if you don't, someone will take it from you. If you don't believe that you can, then you won't. If you don't believe in yourself, then you can't. Lose the self-pity. Lose the doubt. Build that confidence, and you'll create that monster of success. Never let anyone take away your...

Confidence.

You want the key to confidence?

BE BOLD
AND
BE BRAVE!

Stake Your Flag

Bravery is a mountainous concept.
It's performing to the best of your ability,
knowing one wrong step could send you off
the mountain you were so eager to conquer.
Just when you thought you've overcome your fears
and you could let out a sigh of relief,
you're challenged to maintain that bravery.
No worries though,
you know yourself—
You've been tried and sure have been tested.
The time still hasn't come where you've been bested.
You've come far too high up the mountain
to not give all you do, your own due diligence.
For, a trial made easy is no trial at all,
but those that challenge you to be your bravest,
are those that build you up to be your greatest.
Understand, there's always something you'll face
even after you demolished the struggle
you pegged to the wall just yesterday.
When these moments occur, dig deeper than ever before—
So far down inside of you that you're able to manifest the courage,
maintaining that 'stake your flag on top of the mountain' mentality.
The mentality that you are so confident
that your obstacles have no other choice
but to tremble within the presence of your bravery.

Share Your Story
About The
#Confidence_Foothold
@The_Foothold

Scan and Watch
Author Reading
and Commentary

Make A Name
For Yourself

Legacy
'This is all we've got'

Give it your all. This is the only chance you have. One life. One opportunity. To prove your worth. To be remembered. To make a name for yourself. We can't take this lightly. So many people every day lose their lives. Some before they even get a chance to prove themselves. Some after it's too late. That isn't you! You still have time! You still have a chance! Even though time isn't on anyone's side. There's still time. Someone somewhere will remember you. What will they see when they see your memory? A simple person? A selfish human? A hero? A relic? Who can you be if you just put it to the front end of your life rather than the rear end? Too often people allow their lives to pass them by. Thinking they'll never be remembered, or amount to anything. This just isn't true. You're different. You're capable of great things. You have the ability to affect the lives of everyone around you. Everyone does. You don't have to be famous. You don't have to change the world entirely. You just need to change YOUR world for the better. Be a crutch for the less fortunate. Be a role model for those who didn't have the right example in their lives. Be a person of extraordinary measures. When you think you want it, go for it! When you know you want it, take it! We can't just sit around expecting to be who everyone else wants to be. In fact, we shouldn't even care about being someone everyone else wants to be. We need to just be. Be the better person. Be the one who doesn't take life for granted. Be the one who doesn't live selfishly or in vain. We have the strength, and we are worthy of creating our...

Legacy.

What will you leave behind?

Legacy

Lead yourself to a position that
evokes inspiration.
Gather self-confidence and
accentuate your life
choices
you selected to honor your name.

Liberate yourself,
evolve from the
generic,
and become the
charter and foundation for
your family's next generation.

Laud over your
eccentricities, creating
greatness to aspire to be like.
All of those that are great,
championed
years of struggle to succeed.

Leave your love, memories, and
everything
gained and
achieved in your lifetime, with the
chosen ones
you trust to honor your legacy.

Share Your Story
About The
#Legacy_Foothold
@The_Foothold

Scan and Watch
Author Reading
and Commentary

For this life
I am

GRATEFUL

Gratitude

'Can you feel it?'

Now wait. It's not just a feeling. It's an action. It needs to be performed. Not just felt. If we look for gratitude towards ourselves, we'll never find it. It's when we give it that it is endured. Gratitude for workers, partners, employers, leaders. All the hardest people to show your gratitude, is where the real growth resides. If you give it. You will receive it. But you are never to expect it. Or it'll never come to you. Not only does this help us in our work life but personal as well. Relationships grow strong from gratitude. Families prosper with gratitude. Even in the bad times where losses take place. Prove your gratitude for those times and your entire perspective can change. Only then will you be mentally prepared for the worst, which has yet to come. So finally, if you didn't see it coming, here is where I would like to express to you my...

Gratitude.

Thank you!

Be grateful with sincerity.

Thank You

There's so much to be grateful for in this life
and it's imperative that we show and speak of it.
Whether it's between family, friends, coworkers,
or the person who held the door for you.
Simply, show gratitude for being alive.
If I were the moon and you my readers were the sun
I would thank you for being there to rise to the occasion.
You remain there to share my feelings I inscribe onto the page
and for that I am grateful.
If not for you all,
these poems would be lost like notes in an old journal.
But like the sun, you are here.
Rising again, illuminating my path
as I navigate through my inner darkness
and for that,
I will forever be grateful.

Thank you.

Share Your Story
About The
#Gratitude_Foothold
@The_Foothold

Scan and watch
Author reading
And Commentary

TAKE ON

HIGHER

ELEVATIONS

FEET FIRST

From Breakdown to Breakthrough

'Teamwork will make the dream work'

As a team, we had a goal,
you better believe we achieved it.
We did it.
It's done.
But satisfied we will not become.
We won't get lost in the woods.
Our flag has been staked.
Heading back down, driven by desire,
we prepare ourselves to climb again.
This ledge we scale,
we can't outlive forever.
There is no fountain of youth.
Truth be told,
life is a gift we take advantage of in order to sift
through the hardships we face,
the challenges we chase,
and the momentum we pace.
It's demanding.
It's difficult.
It's devastating.
From breakdown to breakthrough.
The foothold to our success was within us.
As a team, we had a goal,
you better believe we achieved it.

Collaborative piece written by Joe and Lauren

Share Your Story
About The
#Teamwork_Foothold
@The_Foothold

Scan and Watch
Author Reading
and Commentary

Need photos done?
Contact Lauren R. Howard
Image Tree LLC

Imagetreellc@gmail.com

The Foothold

The Foothold

Made in the USA
Middletown, DE
25 February 2022

61799662R00106